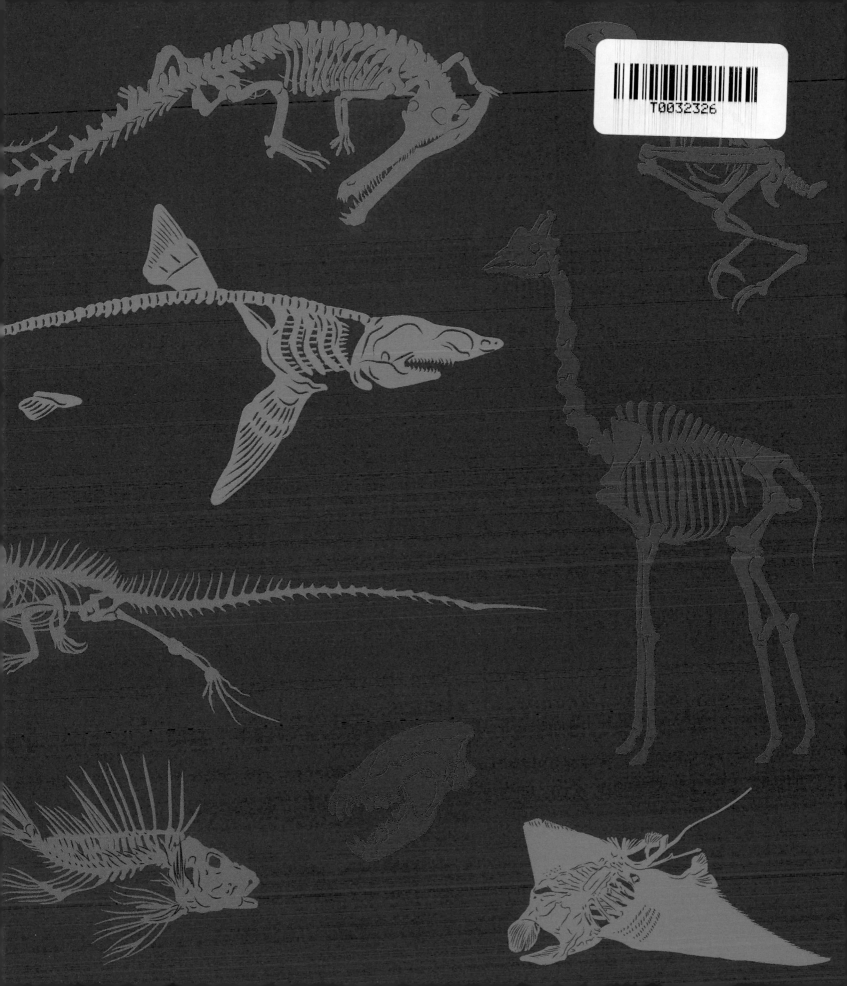

Versatile Vertebrates

Albatros

There are many animal species in the world. Counting just the ones we can find, there are about two million of them. Some are still hidden from us, waiting to be discovered. Sadly, others have already been lost forever.

Clever scientists have ordered these animals into groups to help us understand them better. Vertebrates comprise the biggest group. To be a vertebrate, you need a skeleton, and this skeleton must have a skull and a backbone.

Many different animals are vertebrates, including us humans. If you knock on your own head, the sound you hear is made by your skull. When you see someone with a sore neck or back, the ache is coming from the backbone. The backbone is composed of vertebrae, which cause pain if moved in the wrong way. *Vertebrates* take their name from the *vertebrae*.

We humans are also mammals. Mammalian young are suckled by the mother. All other mammals are vertebrates too. As well as mammals, vertebrates include birds, reptiles, amphibians, fish, and cartilaginous fish. Even though their skeletons are mainly composed of cartilage, cartilaginous fish are vertebrates. We can forgive them this, as they have been in the world for over 500 million years! When fish and cartilaginous fish were first around, Earth was one big ocean. Hard to imagine, isn't it?

While fish and cartilaginous fish have remained in the oceans, they now also swim in lakes, rivers, streams, and ponds too. Some even live in aquariums. Amphibians are happy in water, on land, and underground. Reptiles too. Birds and mammals do as they please in all kinds of places: on land, underground, in the water, and in the air. What all these creatures have in common is their breathing—they need oxygen to live. They also need food. And as they can't be left alone, they must reproduce regularly.

This book doesn't explain what makes humans happiest and what is most important for human life—which is as it should be, because we humans know these things very well already. Instead, this book explains what other vertebrates do and don't enjoy, and it tells us about all the things they can manage. If there's anything you wish to know about vertebrates but fail to find here, go ask a vertebrate—specifically a zookeeper!

Cartilaginous fish

Cartilaginous fish live mainly in the seas and oceans, leaving salt water for fresh water very rarely. A cartilaginous fish has a head, a trunk, and fins. A regular fish has these too, although most fish have skeletons made of bone, whereas cartilaginous fish have skeletons made of—you guessed it—cartilage. This difference may not be apparent at first sight.

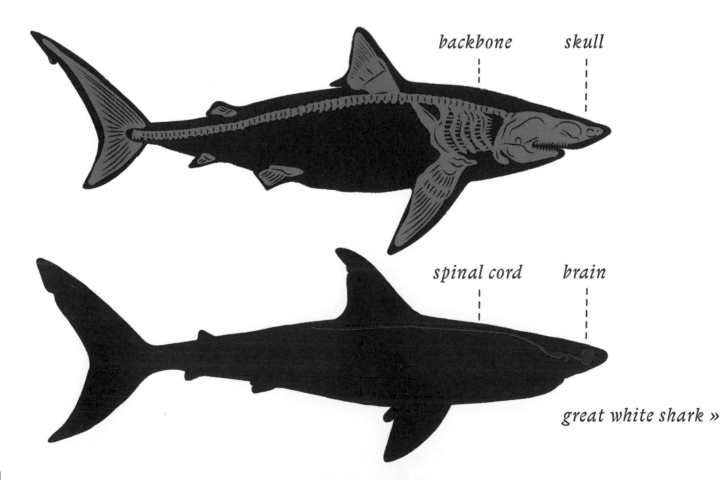

backbone　　skull

spinal cord　　brain

great white shark »

great hammerhead shark

rabbit fish

marbled electric ray

6

Cartilaginous fish come in three basic shapes: fish-shape (e.g., the shark), flat (e.g., the ray), and chimaera shape.

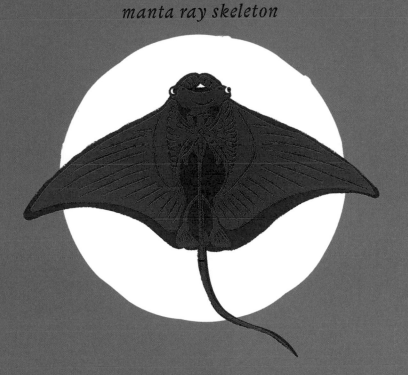

manta ray skeleton

A ray's fins look more like wings. Indeed, a swimming ray looks rather like a bird in flight.

manta rays

*shark's scales
under a microscope*

Cartilaginous fish have hard, bony scales that remind us of teeth. These scales protect the skin. If you were to pet a cartilaginous fish from head to tail, it would feel smooth. If you tried to scratch it, you would find it very difficult!

Sharks are amazing hunters. Although their sight is poor, they have very good hearing and excellent smell. They sense the presence of lunch from some miles away. Their impressive ampullae of Lorenzini (right) pick up the faintest electric signals given out by their prey. The icing on the cake is the lateral line on their bodies, which tells them how deep they are and how much salt water they are surrounded by.

ampullae of Lorenzini

lateral line

a shark's jaws

Apart from the chimaeras, all cartilaginous fish constantly grow teeth. What a pity that we humans can't do the same! Plus, unlike humans, cartilaginous fish grow teeth in several rows.

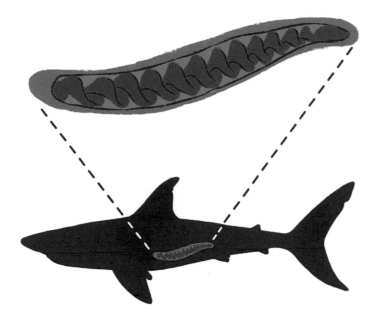

a shark's spiral valve

A shark has a special spiral valve in its stomach, which helps it digest. As its intestines are much shorter than ours, its digestion is slow. In its behind, a shark has a special gland to filter the salt it swallows along with seawater.

Gills look like this.

Cartilaginous fish take oxygen from the water through their gills. In order to breathe, they must swim a lot, as their gills work like a sieve to collect oxygen from the water.

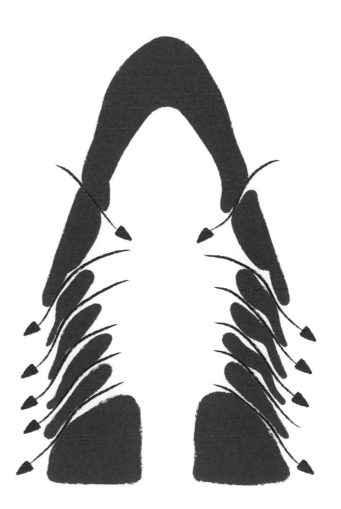

Gills work like this.

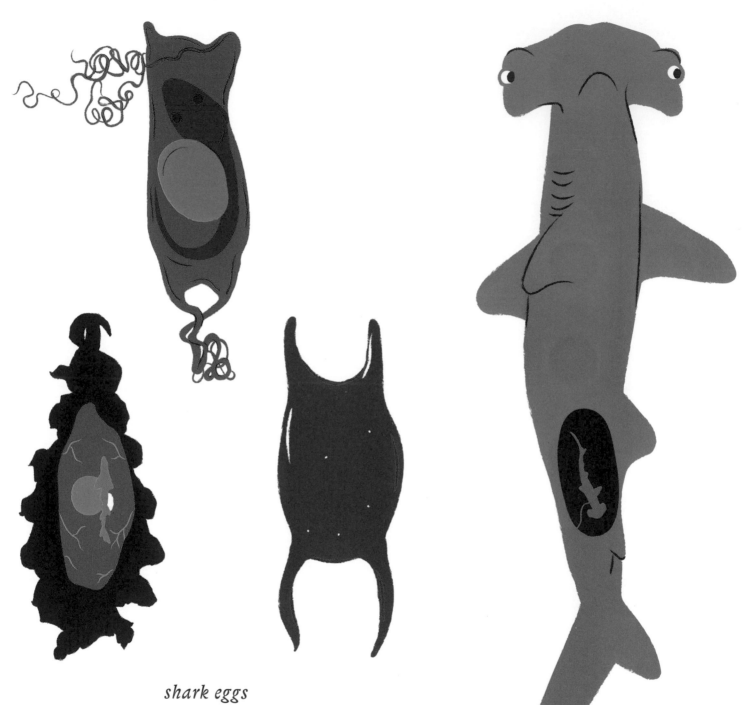

shark eggs

*great hammerhead
shark (female)*

Cartilaginous fish hatch in different ways—
some from eggs outside the mother's body,
others from eggs inside it.

The electric ray is strange among cartilaginous fish, because it doesn't hunt like the others, which swim to their prey. Before eating its prey whole, the electric ray gives it a proper electric shock.

electric ray

Fish

Not all fish live in the salt water of the sea (like the ones on the next page). We also find them in the fresh water of ponds and rivers. Like cartilaginous fish, they have a head, a trunk, and fins. Unlike cartilaginous fish, they can't be categorized by shape, because they come in all kinds. A sunfish looks nothing like an eel, for instance.

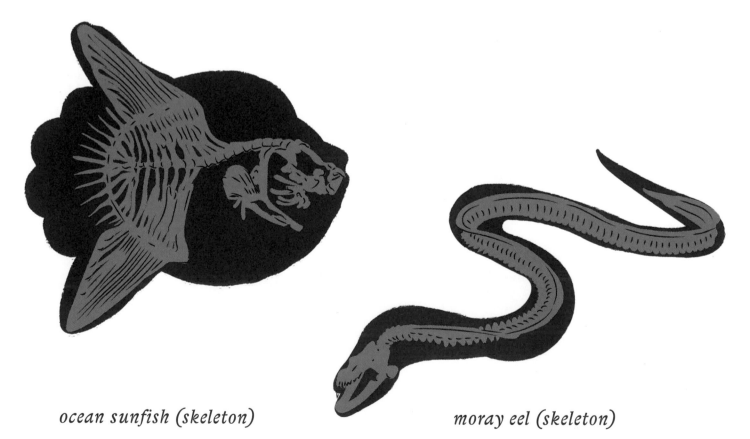

ocean sunfish (skeleton)

moray eel (skeleton)

moray eel

ocean sunfish

anglerfish

red lionfish

swordfish

Fish, too, use their gills to sort oxygen from the water, although their gills are on the inside. To breathe in, a fish fills its mouth with water. To breathe out, it pushes this water through its gills.

salmon breathing through its gills

pike (breathing)

Some fish have learned to breathe in their own way. Pike, for instance, store inhaled oxygen, allowing them to breathe when their mouth is filled with food.

The eel can breathe through its skin—an achievement that allows it to stay on land for hours at a time. Eventually, of course, it must return to the water to keep from drying out.

European eel

This little chap is called the labyrinth fish because of its extra breathing organ, which looks like a maze, also called a labyrinth. This organ allows it to inhale oxygen directly from the air.

labyrinth fish

Siamese fighting fish

lateral line

Fish have sensitive whiskers. These allow them to taste the water around them and to gauge the temperature. Like cartilaginous fish, they have a lateral line by which they tell the strength of the water current. Although their ears are hidden, fish can hear, and they see in color. A fish's eyes contain a water-like liquid, which allows it to see underwater—like humans do, when we go diving with goggles on.

sensitive places on a fish's face

tactile hair

fish skin under a microscope

We shouldn't touch fish. Not because they are slippery and slimy, but because we would harm them. This slipperiness is concealed in glands in the fish's skin. Fish need this slime, which protects their sensitive skin from damage and bacteria, as well as from rascals who would like to catch them in their bare hands.

Their bony scales have a similarly protective purpose. As you can see in the picture below, fish scales vary from species to species. You will also notice that scales have different grooves on them. Like the annual rings of trees, these grooves increase in number with age, thereby allowing us to tell the age of the fish.

round scales of smooth-skinned fish

rhomboid scales of more-evolved fish

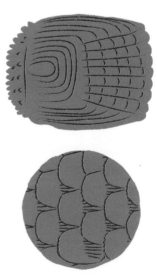

placoid scales of fish with sharp dorsal fin

Fish eggs, too, vary from species to species. Some fish simply spray their eggs into the water. Others might stick them to a rock or plant, and it is from here that the young fish—known as fry—emerge.

fry

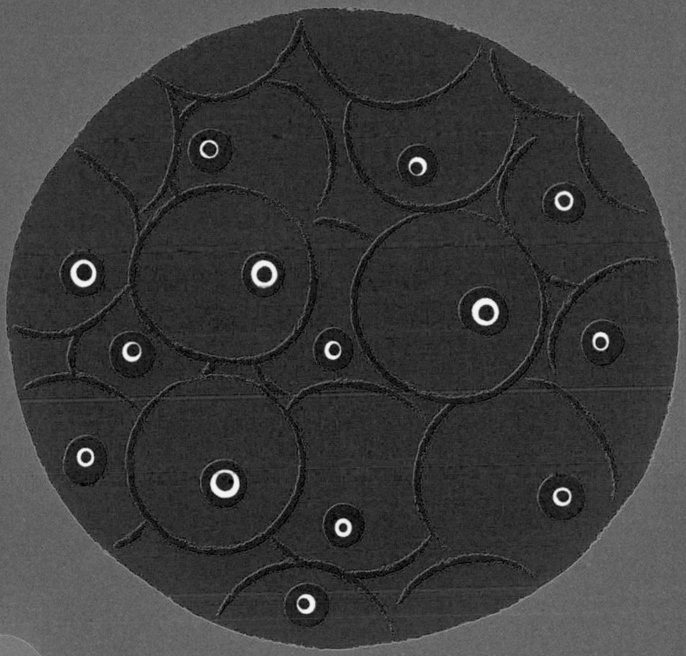

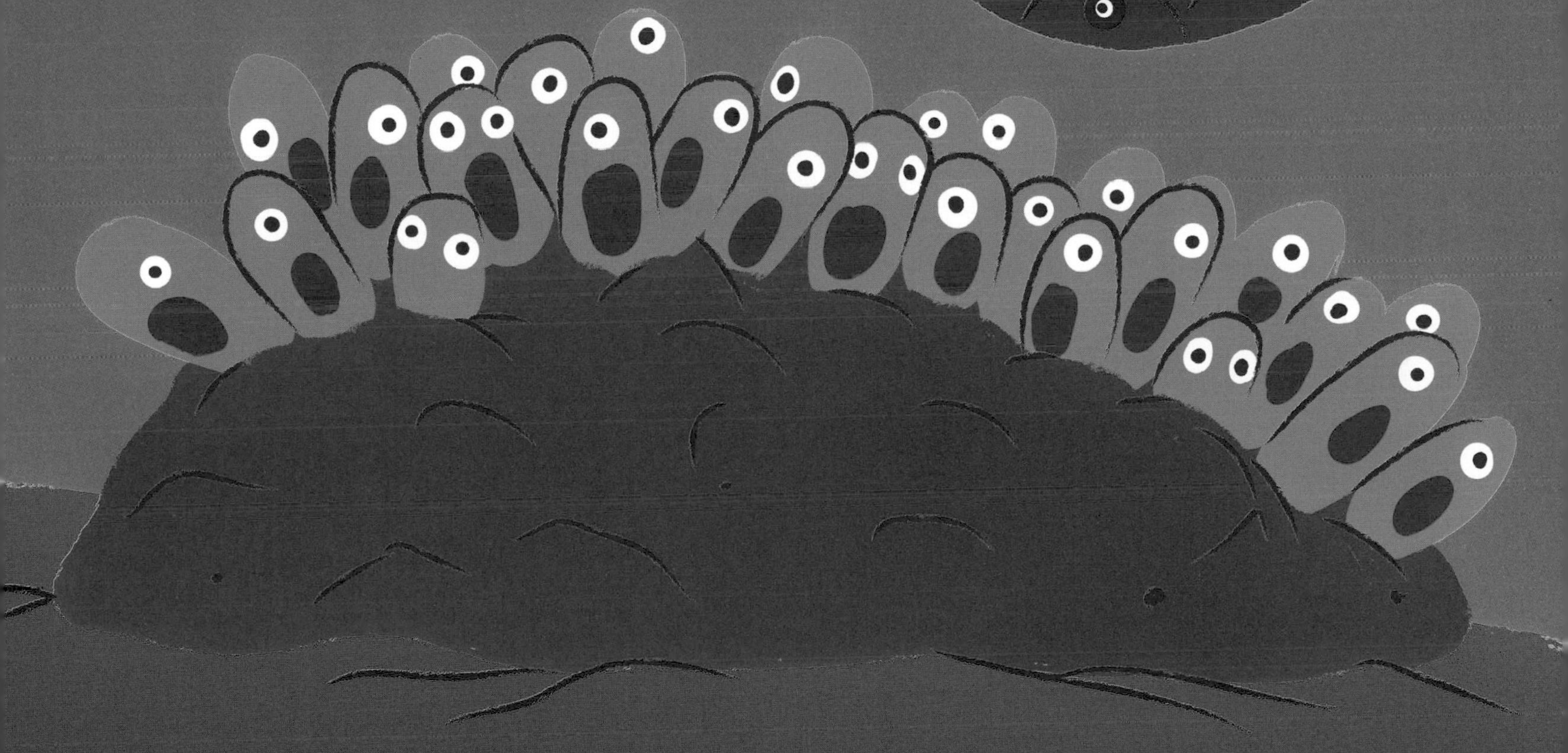

eggs on a rock

Some fish eggs are carried in the mother's belly. In the case of the seahorse, though, the eggs are the father's concern. The mother places them in a pouch on the belly, where they are cared for by the father until they are grown and shoot out of the pouch.

seahorse (male)

fighting fish and bubble nest

That it breathes oxygen from the air isn't the only strange thing about the labyrinth fish. Its newly laid eggs are stuck together so that they look like a floating nest.

The bitterling is so afraid for its eggs that it keeps them safe by hiding them in a shell. To place their eggs, they use a tubular organ called an ovipositor.

bitterling with ovipositor

wood frog

Amphibians

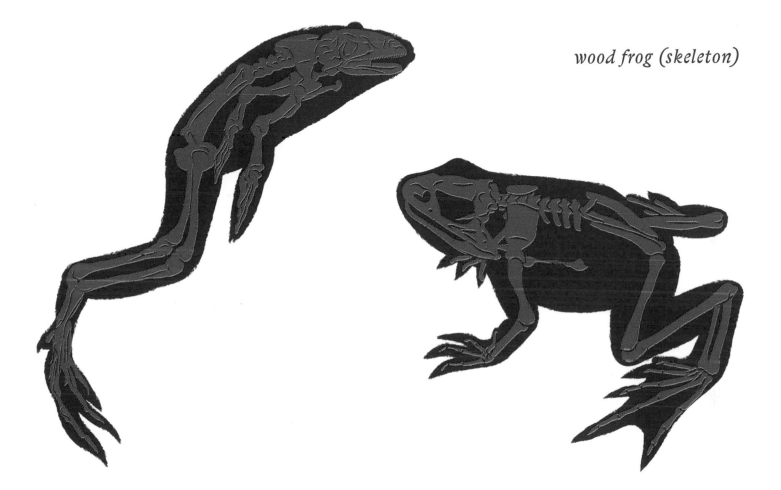

wood frog (skeleton)

We mostly find amphibians on land, but only without their children. Amphibian young stay in the water, and as a result they grow into a special kind of vertebrate. If you search for an amphibian, stay away from saltwater oceans: amphibians are found only in fresh water. Amphibians include frogs. They are easy to recognize by their strong hind legs, thanks to which they can jump great distances.

There are exceptions to this, of course. Caecilians have no legs; they crawl along on their bodies, which are covered in ring-like scales. Unlike fish scales, caecilian scales are made of minerals, not bone. All you need to remember, however, is that caecilians have scales and no legs.

ringed caecilian

No other amphibians have scales. Most have four digits on their front legs and five on their hind legs. The webbing between these digits makes amphibians strong swimmers. The strength in their hind legs makes them powerful jumpers. Flying frogs also have webbing between their toes. When they jump, they spread their webbed toes out like a sail, allowing them to move elegantly from tree to tree.

flying frogs

Amphibians breathe air and absorb water through their smooth skin. This skin, which is periodically shed, is kept moist by subcutaneous glands.

subcutaneous glands under a microscope

fire salamander

poison dart frog

Salamanders and poison dart frogs have venomous glands in their skin. While some such glands do no more than sting, those of the poison dart frog can kill. There's no need to worry, however: the super-toxic poison dart frog lives far away in the rainforest; besides, it is so brightly colored that no one can miss it, allowing everyone to flee in time.

Amphibians are cold-blooded, so freezing conditions are no problem for them. When the weather gets warmer, they simply thaw out. Quite a special way to hibernate, wouldn't you say?

wood frog

wood frog (frozen)

Amphibians have color vision and pretty good eyesight. Frogs even have a third eye on the forehead, although this eye doesn't have color vision; all it does is sense how much the sun is or isn't shining.

frog brain with a third eye

external gills

An adult amphibian breathes through its mouth or skin. To grow, amphibian young must live in water. As they cannot breathe underwater through the mouth or skin, they do so through gills. The gills of a young amphibian are unlike those of a cartilaginous fish or an ordinary fish: they look more like whiskers.

axolotl

red-eyed tree frogs

Have you ever heard frogs croaking after rainfall? Have you ever wondered how such small creatures can make so much noise? What we are hearing are frog dads telling frog moms that the time has come to lay eggs. As you know, eggs need water or damp surroundings, which the rainfall has now provided.

Vocal sac amplifying a frog's croaking

Amphibians lay their eggs in water. Larvae hatch from them. Frog larvae, known as tadpoles, live in water until they develop into adults. An adult amphibian breathes on dry land too, so it is able to leave the water. As a tadpole grows into a frog, it loses its tail. Amphibians have a superpower: they can grow their legs and tail back. The axolotl (the red creature on page 32) is so good at this that it doesn't really age; it can spend its whole life as a larvae. It may not be immortal, but it is forever young.

A salamander mother lays her eggs in water. The larvae that hatch from them grow in the water, eating everything that floats their way, including smaller larvae. Three months of such feasting produces an adult salamander. By the age of three, it is full-grown and able to reproduce. A salamander can live for 20 years in the wild and up to 50 in captivity.

A frog's eggs develop much like a salamander's. Tadpoles have a tail that gradually shrinks. (Humans, too, have the remnants of a tail, where the backside ends.) Having begun eating plants, a tadpole moves on to eating everything else. It grows legs and becomes an adult frog. Frogs reproduce starting at three years of age.

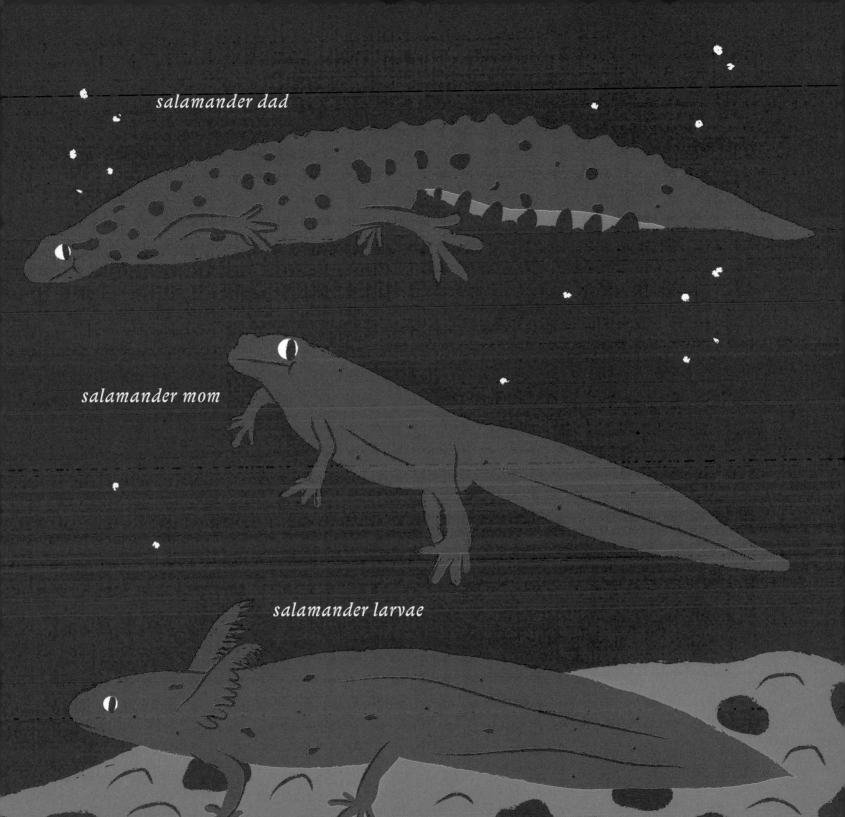

35

Amphibians have a sticky tongue that in many cases can be flicked far out of the mouth. This helps them to hunt their favorite food: insects.

a salamander's "shooting" tongue

The turtle frog uses its hind legs to dig a hole, where it lies in wait for unsuspecting beetles. The frog's tongue shoots out and sticks to the beetles, and the poor meal will be in the frog's tummy before it knows what has happened.

Reptiles

Reptiles were the first vertebrates adapted for life on dry land—although some reptiles had a change of heart and now live only in the water. As the case may be, reptile eggs do better in dry conditions. Like amphibians, reptiles are cold-blooded. Many creatures can be identified as reptiles by the five clawed digits at the end of their legs. Snakes, too, are reptiles, although they have no legs and get about by crawling.

« king cobra

king cobra (skeleton)

Reptiles come in many shapes and sizes. A 20-foot-long crocodile is a reptile, as is a coin-sized chameleon. Because of all these different body shapes, we divide them into lizards (with four legs and a tail), snakes (legless), and turtles (with a carapace).

giant turtle

sea krait

Although sea snakes live underwater, they breathe with their lungs, as we do. For this reason, from time to time they must come to the surface for air.

flying dragon in flight

42

flying dragon inside

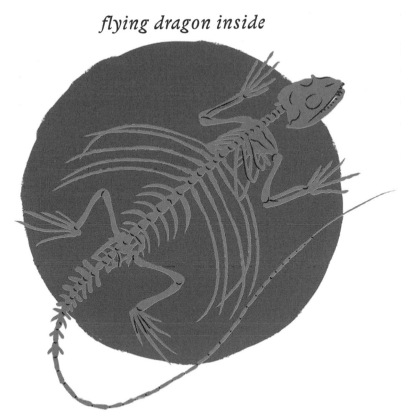

The flying dragon is the last gliding reptile on Earth. It needs no wings to fly; the patagia membranes on the sides of its body perform this function. When it jumps from a tree, the flying dragon spreads its patagia and travels on the wind like a paper kite. Green basilisks, also known as Jesus Christ lizards, have specially shaped hind legs that allow them to walk on water.

green basilisk

gharials

Gharials have small legs that are specially adapted for swimming, which they do quite well. They have a long, flexible tail with a flattened end, which they use as a paddle. Their skin, too, is adapted for speedy swimming. They rarely use their legs to get about on land.

The thorny devil is thus called
because it is covered with sharp
spines. These ensure that no one
eats it.

thorny devil

reptile skin under a microscope

Many lizards have little bumps in their body. It is common for them to shed their skin—very slowly and in stages. Snakes, meanwhile, shed their whole skin at once, thus leaving behind an empty, see-through "snake" of old skin.

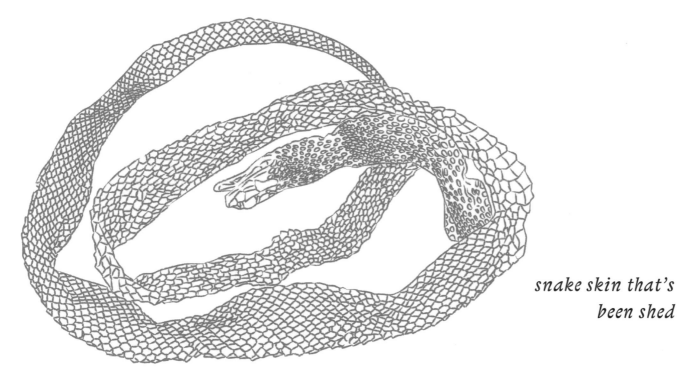

snake skin that's been shed

« panther chameleons

Chameleons have special skin that changes color. Often, the change depends on their mood—it lets others know what they are or aren't keen to do. A chameleon can also change color to fit in with its surroundings, when basically it disappears.

Geckos have sticky pads on their toes, which they use to cling to trees as they sprint up and down them. Geckos, turtles, and crocodiles are the only reptiles that produce a sound. The call of the gecko sounds like a loud dog bark.

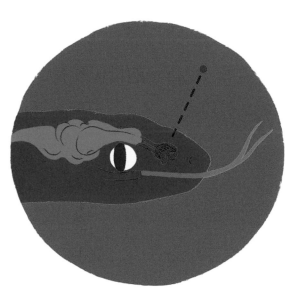

a snake's Jacobson organ

As reptiles are more or less deaf (snakes entirely so), they are heavily reliant on sight and smell. Some—notably snakes—have a so-called Jacobson organ, which combines taste and smell. Because of this, snakes can use their tongue to catch various scents. This may either lead them to their prey or warn them of danger.

tokay gecko

With few exceptions, reptiles are born from eggs. Some of these eggs have a hard shell, some a soft one. Young reptiles emerge from both with the help of an egg tooth. This tooth's only use is to break the shell; in time, it simply falls off—rather like our baby teeth.

crocodile egg (hard)

snake egg (soft)

the tuatara's third eye

The tuatara has a stunted, sightless third eye on top of its head.
Like the third eye of a frog, its only function is to tell how much light there is outside.

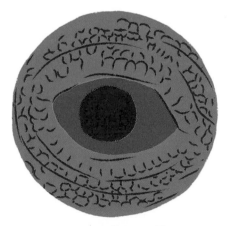

narrow pupil

round pupil

Reptiles have good vision, and their eyes have a third lid. Pupil shape varies from species to species. Nocturnal snakes (awake at nighttime) have narrow pupils, while diurnal snakes (awake in daytime) have round ones. Nocturnal snakes need these narrow pupils, which let less light into the eyes, to keep from going blind if they wake during the day.

Although crocodiles live in the water,
they hunt on dry land. So that they can
lie in wait in the water while seeing
and hearing what is going on above
the surface, their eyes and ears are on
the top of their head.

Nile crocodile

Birds

Birds are the first warm-blooded vertebrates we have encountered in this book. Being warm-blooded means being able to change your body temperature and to thereby adapt to your surroundings. Because of this ability, we find birds all over the world. Most birds have the great advantage of flight; instead of front legs, they have wings. Birds can fly long distances at high speeds. The falcon, for instance, can reach a speed of over 200 miles per hour. As a bird of prey, it must descend on its prey from a great height, a feat made easier by its tapered wings and keen senses. A falcon in the sky can spot a little mouse in a field!

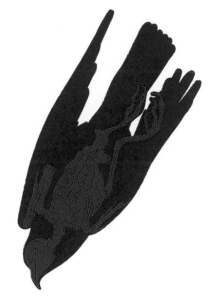

peregrine falcon (skeleton)

The hummingbird does not hunt. Instead, it feeds on flower nectar. When a hummingbird flaps its wings, it does so to remain in one place. The fluttering of the wings is so fast that we don't even see them move—a feat that the hummingbird achieves thanks to its powerful chest muscles. All flight-capable birds have such muscles, as well as a strong yet lightweight skeleton.

tongue and pectoral muscles

bird lungs with air sacs

Birds are so light because they have small lungs. They do much of their breathing by means of large air sacs that lift the bird's body, regulate its temperature, and help it produce different sounds. Birds have a sound-producing organ called a syrinx, which allows them to communicate with each other by the faintest tweet or the most magnificent birdsong.

syrinx

gentoo penguin
(skeleton)

The penguin exchanged its wings for fins. The webbing between its toes makes it the fastest swimmer of all birds: it swims at speeds of up to 20 miles per hour (about three times faster than the quickest human swimmer).

gentoo penguins

Paleognaths (such as ostriches, kiwis, and emus) may have stunted wings, but they also have strong legs to compensate. These legs make them very fast runners. African ostriches run at speeds of up to 55 miles per hour, the average speed of a car!

ostrich

webbed foot of an aquatic bird

foot of a bird of prey

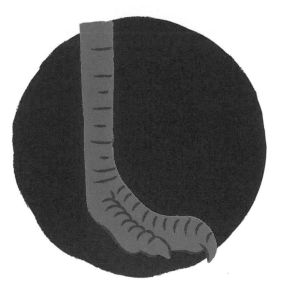

foot of a paleognath (without a hind toe)

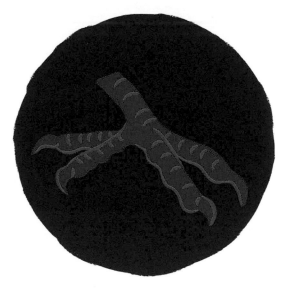

foot of a woodpecker

The legs of different bird species have adapted to their surroundings. Most bird's feet have four toes, which change position to help the bird hunt, swim, run, and climb.

pileated woodpecker

tongue of a pileated woodpecker

Woodpeckers clutch a tree with their toes, braced by their tail feathers, as they use their strong beak to peck holes in it. From these holes, their long tongue will pull beetles and grubs to feed on. To rid the trees of these unwanted inhabitants without hurting itself, a woodpecker must have a strong neck and skull

I am sure you have seen a pigeon before, but have you seen a pigeon feeding its young? Birds (pigeons included) have a special pouch in the throat known as a crop, where good parents store pre-digested food for their children.

domestic pigeons

Pelicans feed by swooping down, opening their beak, scooping fish from the water as you would scoop up the noodles in your soup, then storing their catch in a large pouch under the beak. This strategy is like a fisherman with his net.

white pelican with pouch
filled with fish

Another aquatic bird is the goose. It gathers food using its specially adapted beak to strain out the water. A goose's feathers are adapted for the water. To stay dry, geese, ducks, and other aquatic birds grease their feathers. Greasy feathers don't take on water.

Wet feathers are heavy. Heavy feathers make a heavy bird, which can't fly well. Feathers are very important for a bird, who must change them regularly. A goose sheds its feathers all at once. Until they grow back, it can't fly. That's right: you won't see a wet bird or a naked bird in flight.

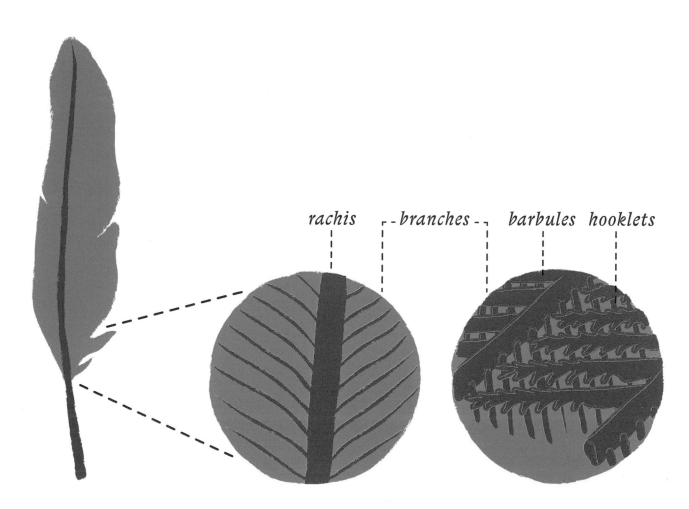

A bird's feather

A feather is composed of a rachis and branches.

The branches of a feather comprise hooklets and barbules.

domestic goose

brown kiwi

kiwi with egg (skeleton)

The kiwi is an endemic animal—meaning they all live in the same place: New Zealand. For a long time, New Zealand had no predators, so there was no taste for kiwi meat. As a result, the kiwi became so relaxed that it simply stopped flying. Like all other birds, it is born from an egg. As a kiwi egg contains a lot of yolk, it is unusually large. The yolk develops into an embryo, which develops into a young bird. Because of the large amount of yolk, a newborn kiwi is already pretty big. No one knows why this is the case, and the kiwi sure doesn't care.

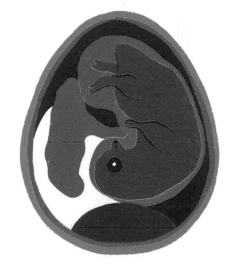

In a kiwi egg, the transformation of yolk into embryo takes 2–3 months.

Mammals

Mammals are warm-blooded animals too. In most cases they have four legs, a head, a tail, and a body covered in hair or fur. Unlike the other creatures in this book, newborn mammals feed on their mother's milk. They grow into weird and wonderful shapes and sizes, and they are found all over the world—in the water, in the air, on and under the land, even in your home. Their bodies adapt to their environment. The huge giraffe, for instance, has a long neck so as to reach the leaves of trees in the extreme African heat. Even so, like all other mammals—including you, including your teacher—the giraffe has only seven neck vertebrae.

« reticulated giraffe

reticulated giraffe (skeleton)

webbed feet

As otters live in an aquatic environment, they have webbed feet to help them swim. They have learned to use these feet to open their favorite food: clams.

sea otters

Hyenas are scavengers. Scavengers feed on the dead bodies of other predators, so they are hardly picky eaters. Fortunately, the hyena has strong jaws that enable it to eat any kind of leftovers—even bones!

skull of a spotted hyena

whole spotted hyena

Over time, the legs of the seal
evolved into flippers, allowing it to
spend all day in the water. The ears
and nose of a seal have special flaps
to keep the water out.

harbor seal

Some mammals can fly. The world's largest flying mammal is the megabat. Its wingspan can be as much as 5 feet, 6 Inches—about the height of the author of this book!

megabat in flight

megabat asleep

porcupine (with spines)

stag (with antlers)

The skin of most mammals is covered in hair or fur. Many change their coat with the seasons, as anyone with a pet dog or cat knows. Mammal hair takes many forms. In some animals—the hedgehog or the porcupine, for instance—it has developed into spines. The porcupine can shoot its quills. The skin of some mammals sprouts horns or antlers.

cow (with horns)

Mammals digest their food in the stomach, which is in the abdomen. Cows and other ruminants have more than one stomach—four, to be precise.

cows, or cattle

« chimpanzee

All mammals have a well-developed sense of hearing, sight, smell, touch, and taste, although these abilities vary from species to species. For instance, a monkey recognizes which fruit is ripe by its redness and with the help of the taste buds in its mouth.

Although mammal ears vary greatly in shape, all contain a cochlea with small bones, an eardrum, a malleus, and an anvil. This gives them hearing good enough to perceive sounds such as the buzzing of beetles, the blowing of the wind, birdsong, and even music.

To communicate, mammals make all kinds of sounds by opening and closing the vocal cords in the larynx, which produce the sound when the mammal breathes in. We have also learned to do this—so well that we can speak and sing in many different languages.

We shouldn't forget that we are mammals too. Why not try your senses out on an apple? Bite into it and hear its crunch and relish its taste and smell. Notice its color and how it feels to the touch.

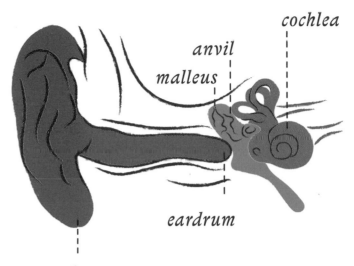

cochlea

anvil

malleus

eardrum

human ear

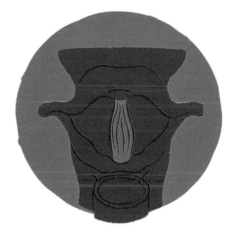

vocal cords closed – silence

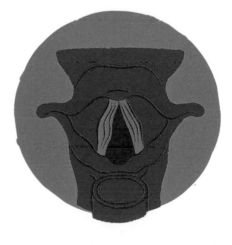

vocal cords open – sound

blue whales – the largest creatures on Earth

Whale songs carry all the way across the ocean. The whale is an aquatic mammal. Unlike the fish and cartilaginous fish that they somewhat resemble, whales must rise to the surface from time to time in order to breathe.

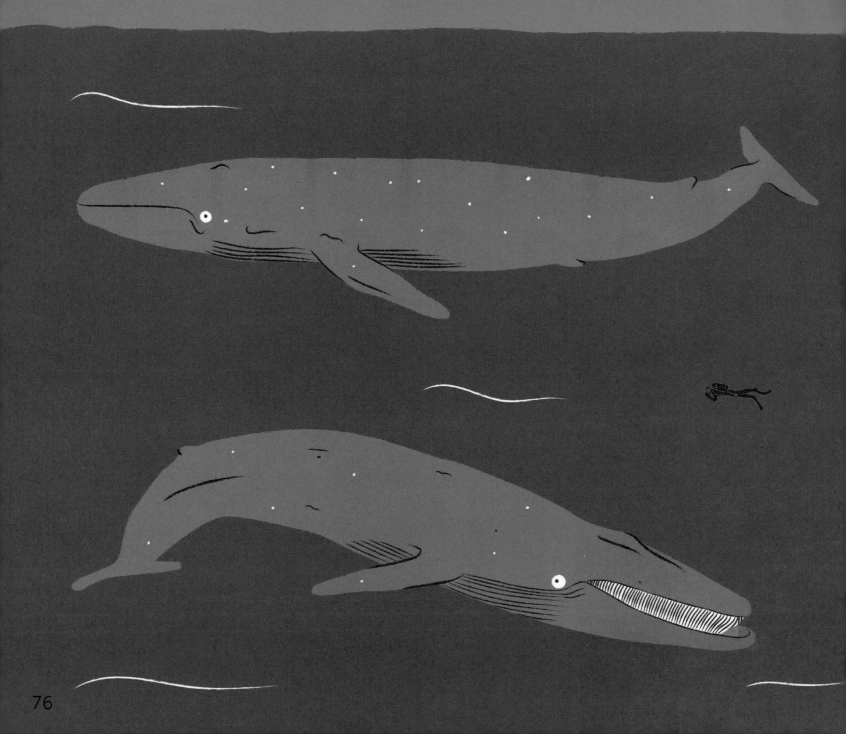

kangaroo and joey

Mammalian young grow in the mother's tummy, not inside an egg. Mammals known as marsupials remain hidden for a while after birth, completing their development in the mother's pouch. The Australian kangaroo continues to take rests in its mother's pouch long after its birth.

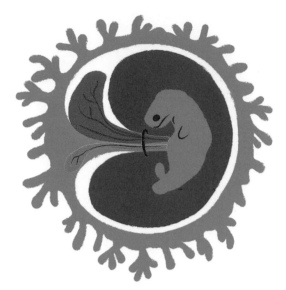

mammal embryo

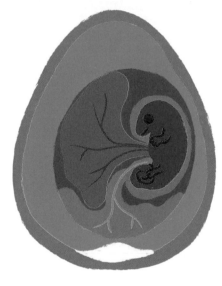

reptile embryo

The mammal embryo develops in the mother's womb, not inside an egg, as is the case with birds. An interesting exception to this is the platypus, which lays eggs like a bird, has a beak like a bird, but after hatching feeds its young with mother's milk.

A platypus mother doesn't feed her young from the breast, like other mammals, however. Her milk flows from grooves on her abdomen. The platypus is one of the few living mammals to produce venom. The venom—which is not lethal, but unpleasant enough— is contained in a spur on a hind foot. If you would like to see a platypus, you must go to eastern Australia— or to the zoo.

© B4U Publishing for Albatros,
an imprint of Albatros Media Group, 2023
5. května 1746/22, Prague 4, Czech Republic
Written by Marie Kotasová Adámková & Tom Velčovský
Illustrated by Barbora Idesová
Translated by Andrew Oakland
Edited by Scott Alexander Jones

Printed in China by Leo Paper Group